WEIRDO 8

REALLY WEIRD!

Scholastic Press
An imprint of Scholastic Australia Pty Limited (ABN 11 000 614 577)
PO Box 579 Gosford NSW 2250
www.scholastic.com.au

Part of the Scholastic Group
Sydney • Auckland • New York • Toronto • London • Mexico City
• New Delhi • Hong Kong • Buenos Aires • Puerto Rico

A catalogue record for this book is available from the National Library of Australia

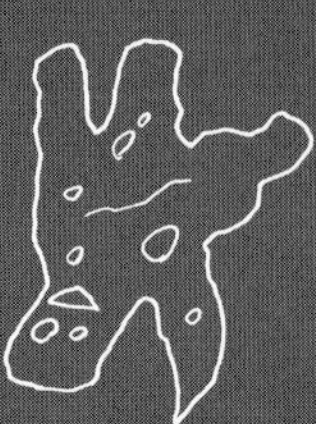

ISBN: 978-93-5471-908-0

Typeset in Grenadine MVB, Push Ups and Lunch Box.

This reprint edition Dec., 2024

ANH DO

Illustrated by JULES FABER

WEIRDO 8

REALLY WEIRD!

A SCHOLASTIC PRESS BOOK
FROM SCHOLASTIC AUSTRALIA

BOOGIE
ON
DOWN!

CHAPTER 1

Our **school dance** was coming up and we were all **REALLY** excited.

Before class, Hans Some was showing off some of his **best** dance moves.

It turns out he's a **really great break-dancer.**

In fact, he's
really,
really
great!

Even Bella thought so.

Hans Some's moves were **so cool** that the **whole class** started trying them!

OWW!

Henry tried **really hard** . . . but he looked like a **dizzy octopus**!

Our school dance was going to be a **BARN DANCE** at the farm, which meant we would pair up for all sorts of **heel-and-toe**

But at the end, we could all dance however we liked!

Maybe I could try **break-dancing**. It couldn't be **that hard**, could it?

If my little brother **Roger** could do it, then surely I could too!

I got ready to show everyone what I could do.

But then I accidentally **stepped on a banana** that had fallen out of my lunch bag!

YOWWWWWWW!

I flew backwards . . .

...and landed **right on my bottom!**

I **spun really fast** around the room!

Everyone thought it was **awesome!**

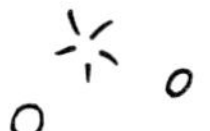

As I was **wobbling around**

Miss Franklin walked in.

'Hello everyone,' she said.

Back at my desk, **James Nott** passed me a note.

'Hey, Weir,' he said. 'Could you please pass this to **Jenny**?'

James was asking Jenny to be his **partner** at the **barn dance!**

I gave it to Jenny, who read the note and nodded at James.

That gave me an idea! I should ask *Bella* to dance with **me**!

I quickly scribbled her a note and passed it to Henry.

Henry passed it to **Mullet** . . .

. . . who passed it to **Toby**

. . . who passed it to **Blake**

. . . who passed it to . . .

Why wasn't **Wendy** passing it to **Bella**?!

Before I could ask her to keep passing the note to Bella, Wendy turned around . . .

Oh no! She thought I was asking **her** to dance with me!

Oh man. Wendy's **GREAT fun** and all, but she **isn't Bella . . .**

At recess, I rushed around looking for Bella to explain to her why I would be dancing with Wendy.

I found her talking to Hans.

Hans **snapped** his fingers and **four white doves** flew across the playground carrying a

big sign!

Bella, will you dance with me?

Oh no!

He was asking her to dance with **him!**

What was she going to say?!

Before Bella could answer, Wendy ran over to her with my note.

'Bella, look!' she said.

'Oh, that's **great**, Wendy,' Bella said. Then she turned to Hans and said . . .

No!

Just when I thought things couldn't get any worse, one of Hans Some's doves **did a big poo on my hair.**

FAST
FOOD!

CHAPTER 2

Road trips are **always exciting** with my family! Especially when we're on our way to collect someone **AWESOME** from the airport!

GRANDMA DO!

Dad **loves to sing songs** on the radio, but he changes the words to **make them funny!**

And Dad always sings **the national anthem** wrong, too.

Yep, ostriches.

MATE, TALK ABOUT FAST FOOD!

Sally loves to play **I SPY**.

'I spy,' said Sally, 'with my little eye, something beginning with . . . **F!**'

That was way too easy.

Farm!

'My turn,' said Dad. 'I spy with my little eye, something beginning with . . . **N!**'

That was too easy as well!

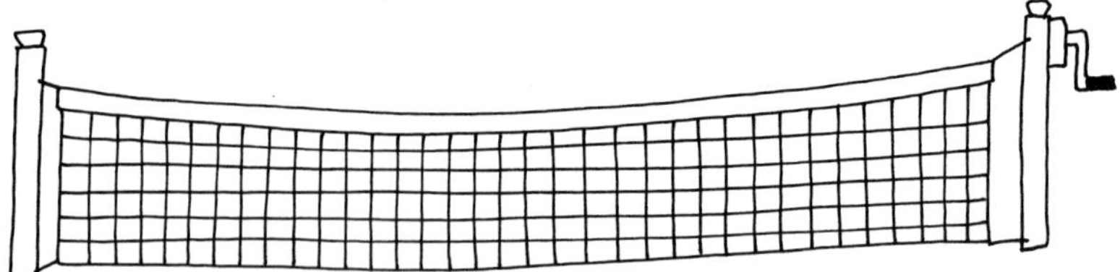

Net!

'No.'

I saw some birds in a tree, and had another guess. **'Nest?'**

'No.'

'Give up?' said Dad. **'Nose!'**

Dad said that when he went **cross-eyed** he could see his **nose**.

Mum was up next.

I SPY WITH MY LITTLE EYE, SOMETHING BEGINNING WITH . . . P!

P? Sally and I were stumped!

Umm.

Pole?

'No.'

Possum?

'No.'

Suddenly Roger cried out.

'Yes, Roger,' said Mum,
'something beginning with **P**.'

'Yes, Roger,' said Mum, '**"P"** is the letter!'

But then Roger pointed to his **pants**.

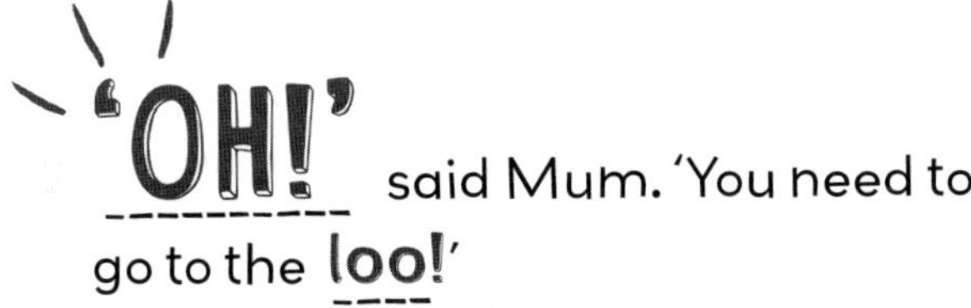

said Mum. 'You need to go to the **loo**!'

Bathroom break!

After we found a bathroom for Roger, we were **back on the road to the airport!**

ARE WE THERE YET?

ARE WE THERE YET?

ARE WE THERE YET?

ARE WE THERE YET?

I spy with my little eye, something beginning with G!

GRANDMA!

BURP!

CHAPTER 3

It was **really good** to see Grandma Do! And it was just in time for **Grandparents Day** at school.

We gave her a **bunch of cards** we'd made.

Then she pulled out a bag **filled with cool presents** for us all!

For Mum and Dad and Granddad, she had a **funny-looking button**.

'Here,' she said, 'try it. It's a **floor bell**.'

A floor bell? Was that for making music with your feet?

'I think you mean **DOOR** bell,' said Dad, giggling.

Sometimes Grandma gets her **English words mixed up!**

SILLY ME.

YES, DOOR BELL!

Mum took the doorbell and pressed the button.

The doorbell **roared like a lion!**

'Press it again!' said Grandma.

This time Dad had a go.

The doorbell started **barking!**

This was the **funniest doorbell** we'd ever heard!

Next, Granddad reached for the doorbell.

'Oops,' said Grandma. 'That was me!'

SORRY!

Sally loved her **cool new diary!** You needed to say the **secret word** to unlock it.

Roger couldn't wait to try out his **Power Paws!**

Just when I thought Grandma might have forgotten me, she said, 'And **lucky last!** Something for Weir!'

What was it going to be?!

'Here you go!' Grandma handed me a pair of **overalls**.

That was a bit of **a weird gift.**

But maybe I could wear them if I ever had to **paint the house.**

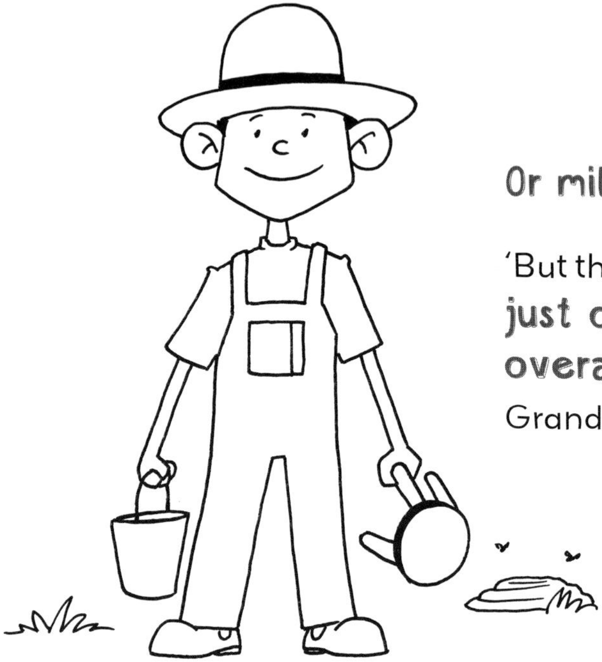

Or milk a cow.

'But they're **not just ordinary overalls!**' said Grandma.

THEY GROW IN THE DARK!

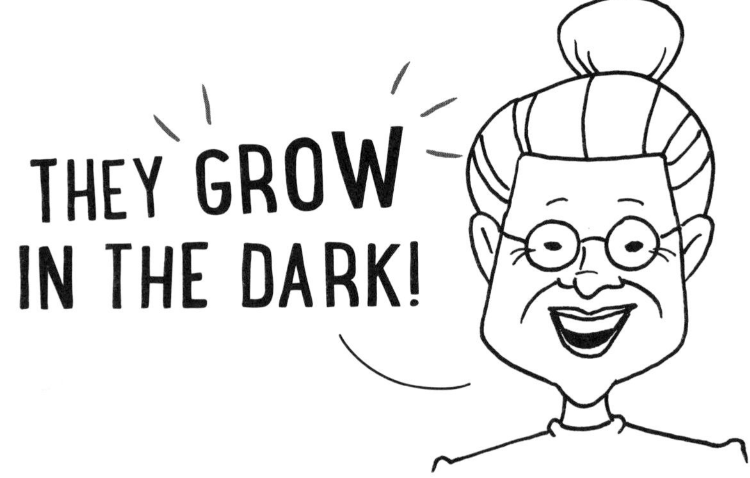

Wow!

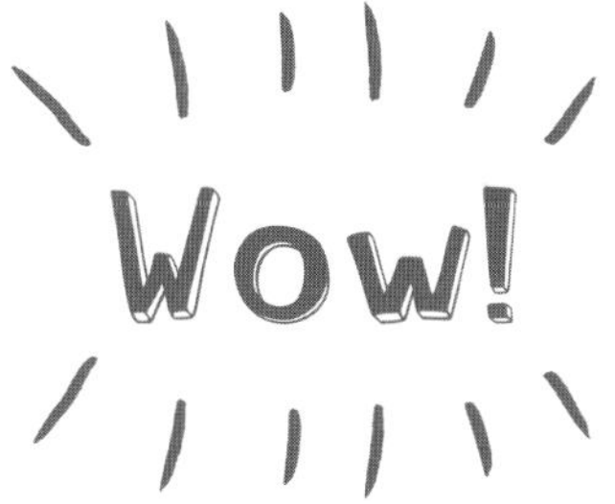

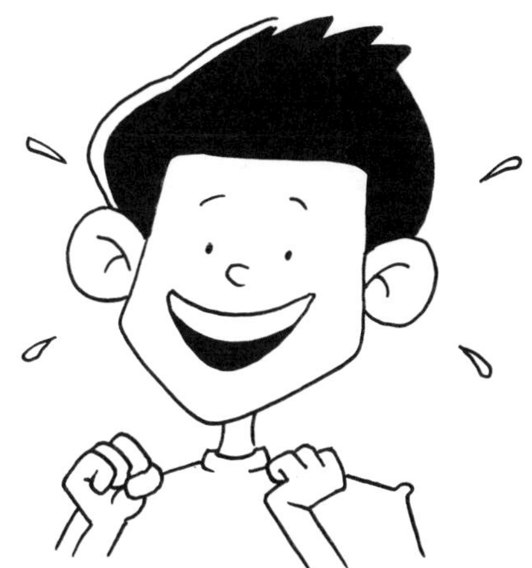

Did that mean I could grow to **ten times** my height?

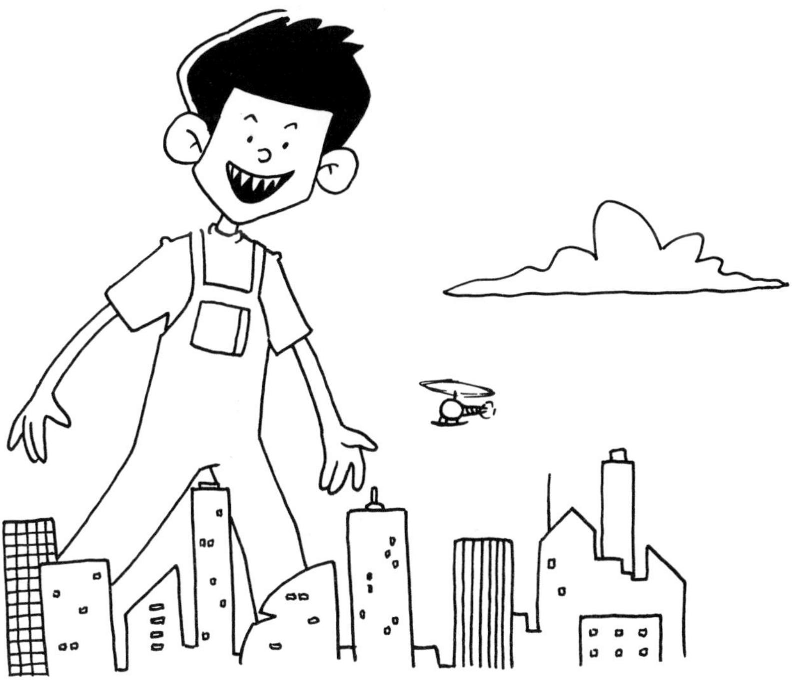

'Oh, silly me,' said Grandma. 'Not GROW,' she said, widening her arms, '. . . **GLOW!** The overalls **GLOW** in the dark!'

I had my own pair of **glow in the dark** overalls!

Just perfect if I ever had to paint the house in the **middle of the night!**

Cool!

YOU MISSED A SPOT!

CLUCK,
CLUCK!

CHAPTER 4

School was filled with people for **Grandparents Day!** Everyone had brought in **home-cooked treats** and things for **show-and-tell.**

There were rows of tables set up for us to share with our grandparents and friends.

Bella and her grandma had baked an **enormous apple pie.** It smelled **delicious!**

It tasted **amazing!**

Hans Some and his **grandfather** had prepared a **lobster** dish.

It looked **very,**

very

fancy.

Wendy and her **Nan** had baked **shortbread cookies.**

'Nan, this is Weir,' said Wendy. 'He's my partner for the **BARN DANCE**!'

'Oh, you're Weir Do!' her Nan said. 'The boy with the **groovy break-dancing move!**'

'I guess that's me,' I said, feeling my **face go red**.

Wendy offered me a cookie.

'Thanks, Wendy,' I said, and took a bite.

'Yum!'

Henry's Poppy loved **gardening.** He was wearing a t-shirt with a picture of a watering-can on it.

It said, **I WET MY PLANTS!**

Poppy had a **big collection** of pet plants . . .

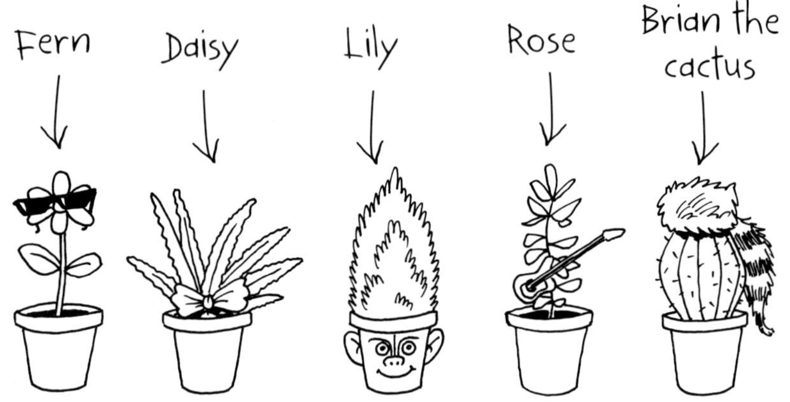

Toby Hogan's **great-uncle** had a collection of **rare coins**. Just as I was about to say hello, they accidentally **dropped a big bucket of them! Oops!**

Granddad was next! He was showing off his **collection of old teeth**, plus he'd cooked up a batch of his **FAMOUS STICKY CARAMEL FUDGE**!

Heaps of people were walking around with their **teeth stuck**!

The fudge was **so** sticky, it could probably **glue a house** together!

FUDGE WON'T BUDGE!

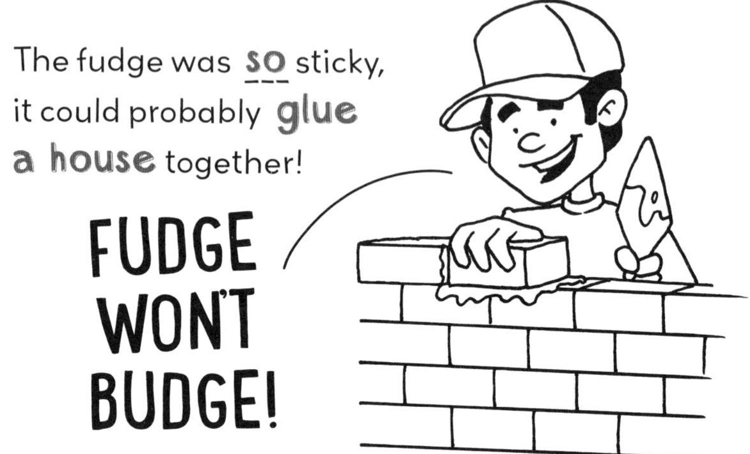

Next in line was Grandma Do, who had **cooked up a storm!** Everything smelled **awesome!**

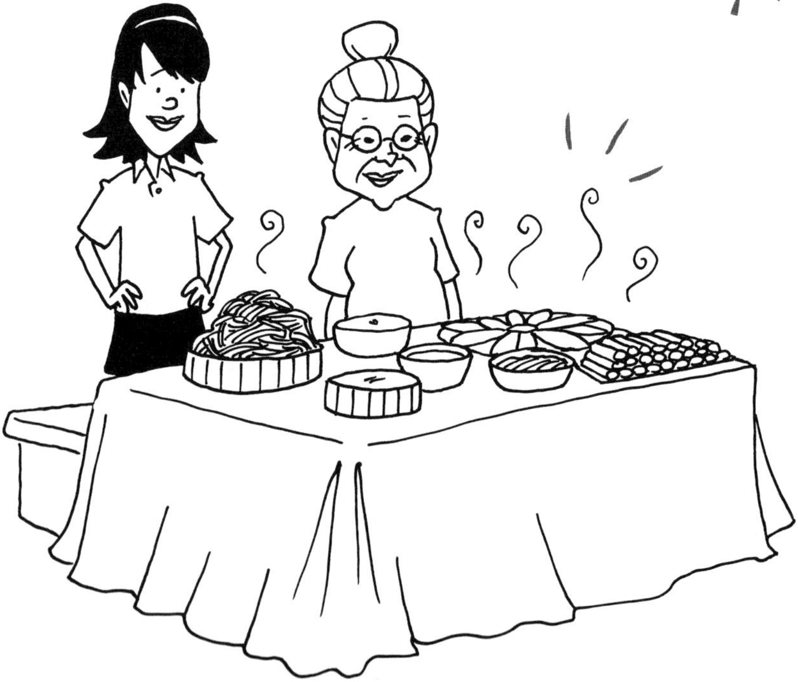

'I'm here!' I said, squeezing behind the table. 'What can I do to help?'

'Everyone's filling up on **cookies** and **pie**!' said Sally. 'I hope they have room left for **Grandma's goodies**!'

'What's that?' asked Mullet, as a few people started gathering around our table.

'I forget what it's called in English,' said Grandma.

And then Grandma acted out what she was trying to say!

'Oh, she means **CRAB!**'
I said.

'What about those?'
asked another kid.

'Um,' said Grandma. 'I forget the word for that too . . .'

So she acted it out again.

'She means **Beef Noodles**!' explained Sally.

'And that one?' asked someone's mum.

'Chicken poo?'
guessed Mullet.

'No,' I said, 'she means **egg!**'

Everyone seemed unsure about the food. Grandma looked a bit sad . . .

'It's all **really yum!**' I called out. 'You should try it! Trust me!'

But no-one would listen.

No-one but Bella!

'Grandma Do! I'm Weir's friend, Bella,' said Bella.

'Oh, **Bella Allen**!' said Grandma, giving her a hug. 'Weir **never stops** talking about you!'

Oh man . . .

It was true, I **did** talk a lot about Bella. But right now I wished I could **hide under the tablecloth!**

'Grandma Do,' said Bella, 'Weir never stops talking about **YOU**! I've heard all about how you like to surprise people in your **gorilla costume**!'

Grandma laughed. 'You never know, I might have brought that costume with me in my **fruitcase**!'

'**SUIT** case!' said Grandma. 'Oops. I keep mixing up my words!'

'You're **so funny**!' said Bella. **'Just like Weir!'**

Now they **both** had me blushing! I **REALLY** wanted to hide under the tablecloth.

'Mmm, this is delicious!' said Bella.

I looked up and saw that Bella was eating one of Grandma's crab rolls. In fact, she was eating **TWO** crab rolls!

'Here, try these,' said Grandma, handing Bella a bowl of noodles and an egg tart.

THESE NOODLES ARE
YUMMY!
AND THESE EGG TARTS!
WOW!

All of a sudden **a whole heap** of people rushed to our table. Everyone wanted to try Grandma's cooking!

SO TASTY!

YUM!

OOH!

DELICIOUS!

In moments . . . the table was **empty**!

Turns out

EVERYONE

loves Vietnamese food!

In the afternoon, there was a **knitting demonstration**.

All the grandparents lined up like **lean, mean knitting machines**! Wool was **wriggling** everywhere!

Bella's grandma was knitting a jumper.

Wendy's Nan was knitting a ***really*** long scarf.

Henry's Poppy was knitting a little beanie (for Brian, the cactus).

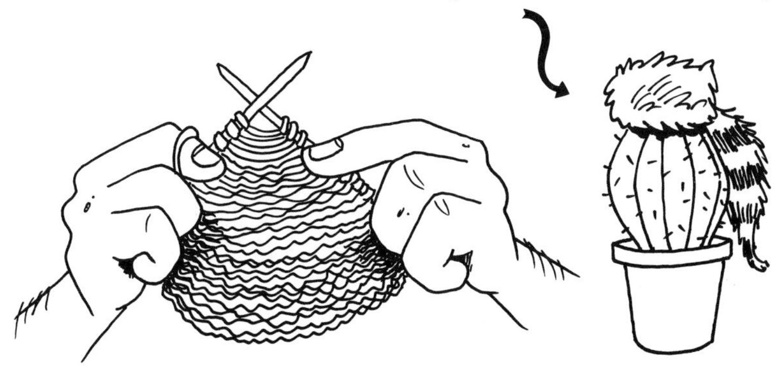

Then I noticed **Grandma Do**.

She had a pair of knitting needles, too . . .

. . . but she was using them like **chopsticks**!

To eat noodles!

That night I was telling Dad all about how much everyone at school **LOVED** Grandma's cooking.

'After Bella started eating it, there was a **mad rush** to our table!' I said. 'It was **crazy**!'

THAT'S BECAUSE GRANDMA'S COOKING IS THE BEST!

'But afterwards, there was a knitting demonstration,' I said. 'Everyone was making **awesome stuff** ... but Grandma was using her knitting needles to **EAT NOODLES**!'

'It was **funny** ...' I said, 'but a bit **embarrassing**, too.'

Just then, I noticed Grandma shuffling away from the doorway.

She must have heard me say that **she'd embarrassed me!**

'Why don't you ask her to join you for your **farm trip** tomorrow?' said Dad. 'That might make her feel better.'

She could visit the farm with my class, then be there for the **barn dance** afterwards!

Then she'd know for sure that **I'm not really embarrassed** by the **funny things** she does!

MILK
SHAKE!

CHAPTER 5

Grandma was **really excited** to be coming with me and my class to the farm. I wore the overalls she gave me to make her **even happier**!

Turns out she had a **matching pair**!

Some of the other grandparents had come along too.

First stop of the day was the cow shed. **Farmer Jo** was going to show us how to **milk the cows**!

To get there, we all walked through the farm gates, along a **very muddy bank**, past a **field of sheep**, and around the **big barn**.

Henry's Poppy wasn't very good at getting the **milk in the bucket**. In fact, most of it **ended up on Henry**!

Henry **shook like a dog** to get it all off him.

Bella and her grandma were a bit better at it. But after a long time, they **only had a few drops.**

Grandma said she had a **secret way** to make cows give lots of milk.

Grandma Do and I

buckets!

Everyone was
really impressed.

'Hey,' said Henry. 'Why did the cow cross the road?'

'Great work, guys,' said Farmer Jo. 'Now let's go and collect some **fresh farm eggs**!'

The chicken coop was **really cool**. The nesting boxes kind of looked like **a whole bunch of bunk beds**.

That could be fun!

Farmer Jo gave us baskets and showed us how to pick up the eggs. You had to be **really careful**, so you **didn't upset the chickens**. It was like being a **super egg ninja**.

Bella and her grandma were really good at being gentle.

Actually, most people were pretty good at it.

But Henry and his Poppy . . .

... had feathers flying everywhere!

Finally they found **one egg** ... but then Henry **dropped it**!

OOPS.

CRACK!
SMASH!
SPLAT!

'That's not **EGG-xactly** what I wanted to happen,' said Henry.

YOU CRACK ME UP!

HAHA! HAHA!

Before long, Grandma and I had collected **a whole dozen**! Grandma was **so awesome**, the hens were almost giving us their eggs.

'Great work, you two,' said Farmer Jo.

Grandma had a farm in Vietnam, so **OF COURSE** she was **awesome** at this stuff.

After visiting the **chicken coop**, we all headed over to **feed the pigs.**

But when we reached the **pig pen** ... it was **empty**!

Farmer Jo cried out! 'They've escaped! Someone must have left the gate open!'

OINK,
OINK!

CHAPTER 6

Where could the pigs have gone? Maybe they'd **caught a bus** somewhere?

Or run away to **join the ballet**?

Or maybe they were just **tired of being pigs** and wanted to **try something else**?

Like being **roosters**!

OINK-A-DOODLE-DO

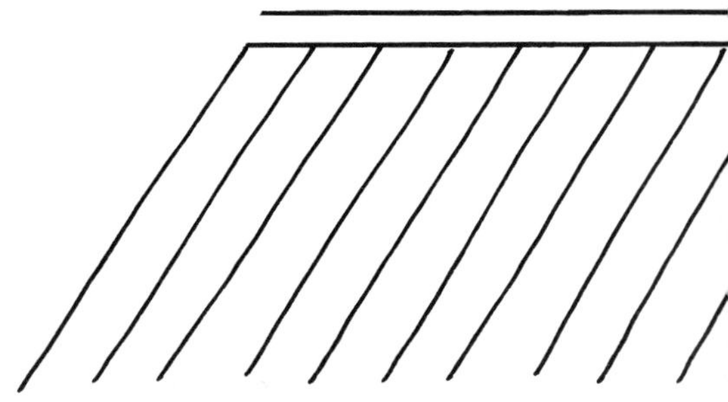

OOOO!

Farmer Jo said they couldn't have gone far, so we were all going to **help with the search**.

A group led by Henry and his Poppy headed up towards the **fruit trees**.

Another group led by Farmer Jo headed around to the **horse stables**.

'Where should we look?' I asked Grandma. It seemed like she had an **idea**.

'What do you know about pigs, Weir?' she asked me.

'Um, they're kind of **round** and they have **big snouts.**'

'What else?' said Grandma.

'They have **wiggly tails** . . .'

'That's true,' said Grandma. 'But what do they **LIKE** most of all?'

'Exactly!' said Grandma. 'Just like the mud we walked through near the farm gate!'

Pigs **LOVE** mud!

Grandma Do was a **GENIUS!**

The pigs were having **so much fun** splashing around in the mud together.

SPLASH!

But once we told them it was **DINNER TIME** they were happy to

follow us

back to

their pen.

COME ON,
LITTLE
PIGGIES!

Farmer Jo was **thrilled** to see us all!

'You found them!' she cried. 'Thank you **so much**!'

Everyone else **cheered**.

Once the pigs were all back in the pen . . . it was **feeding time**!

It was a **feeding frenzy**! Just like everyone eating Grandma's food yesterday!

That must have been some **good slop**!

HEEL-
AND-
TOE!

CHAPTER 7

We'd milked the cows, collected the eggs, fed the pigs . . . and now it was finally time for the **BARN DANCE!**

ONE, TWO,
THREE, FOUR!
SWING YOUR PARTNER
ROUND THE FLOOR!

Wendy and I were having **heaps of fun** dancing the **heel-and-toe**!

Hans and Bella looked like they were having a great time too.

Although I don't remember learning **that barn dance move . . .**

Henry **spun** his partner around **so fast** that she looked like a **tornado**!

WHOOOOOOO

OOOOOOO

OSH!

Miss Franklin and her helpers were having fun watching us.

Even the **farm animals** came for a look.

Wendy suddenly tugged on my arm. 'Weir,' she said, 'do you mind if I go ask **Henry** to dance with me?'

'Go for it!' I said. 'I'm sure he'd love to take you for a spin!'

NICE
MOOOVES!

Henry and Wendy made **great partners**! They both knew how to make each other **laugh**, and they both liked to **whirl around really fast**!

Meanwhile, Hans was dancing with Henry's partner . . . which left Bella **alone!**

This was my chance!

I had to go talk to her!

HI BELLA.
DO YOU THINK YOU'D
MAYBE . . . UM . . .
LIKE TO DANCE
WITH ME?

Bella smiled instantly.

GREAT!

But just as we were about to start . . .

. . . the lights went out!

The barn was in **complete** darkness!

'BLACKOUT!' someone shouted.

'I can't see!' someone else shouted.

Suddenly I noticed a **glow** around me. Where was it coming from?

Me!

It was coming from my **glow-in-the-dark overalls**!

'Hey, look at Weir!' someone called out. 'He's **glowing like a disco ball**! His grandma, too!'

Grandma Do hopped over to me. She was glowing as **brightly** as I was!

Henry called out, 'Hey Weir, I always knew you were one of the **brightest** students in the class!'

The band picked up the music again, and everyone rushed back to the dancefloor, **busting moves** around us.

Me and Bella joined in. Grandma too.

I even showed Grandma my cool break-dancing move.

We were having the best time ever. **Everyone was!**

And me and Bella and Grandma just **kept on dancing** right in the middle of it all!

NOODLES!

CHAPTER 8

We all sat around the table as I told everyone about our fun day on the farm, and **AWESOME** night at the **BARN DANCE**.

'Our **glow-in-the-dark overalls** really saved the day!' I said.

'Hey, where's Grandma?' I asked.

On the table was an **ABSOLUTELY ENORMOUS** bowl of noodles—the **BIGGEST** we'd ever seen.

But Grandma was **nowhere to be found.**

All of a sudden the bowl of noodles **started moving.**

SURPRISE!

AAH!

AAH!

AAAHHH!!

GRANDMA!

FROM ANH

For Kem and Noah!

ACKNOWLEDGEMENTS

For **Beck Young** and **Brian Cook**, whose genius makes my job so much easier.

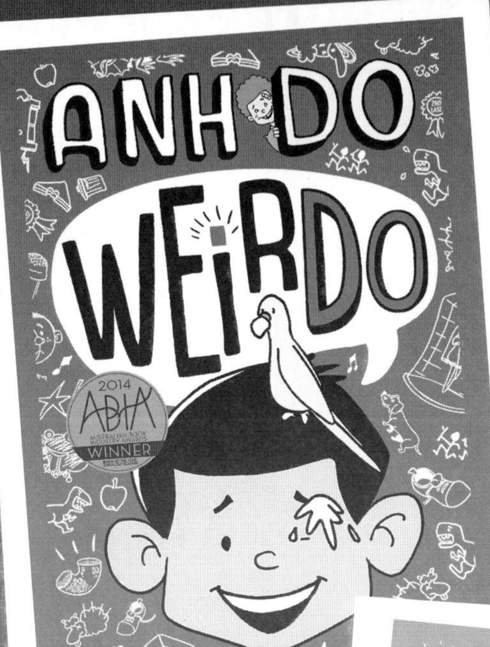

AUSTRALIAN BOOK INDUSTRY AWARDS WINNER!

Book 1

GOT IT!

COLLECT THEM ALL!

Book 3

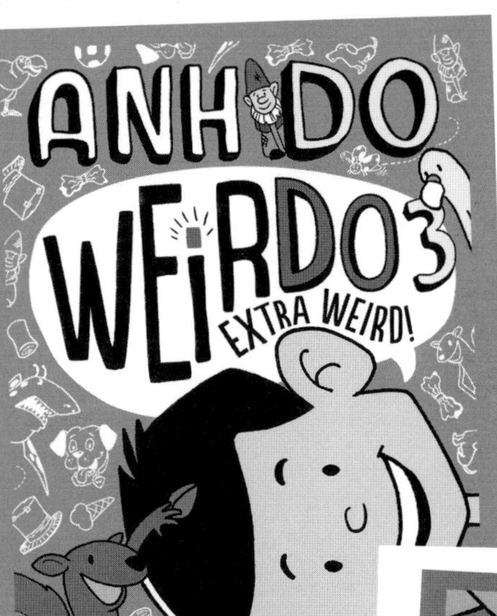

GOT IT!

Book 4

ANH DO

WEIRDO 5

TOTALLY WEIRD!

SCHOLASTIC

Book 5

GOT IT!

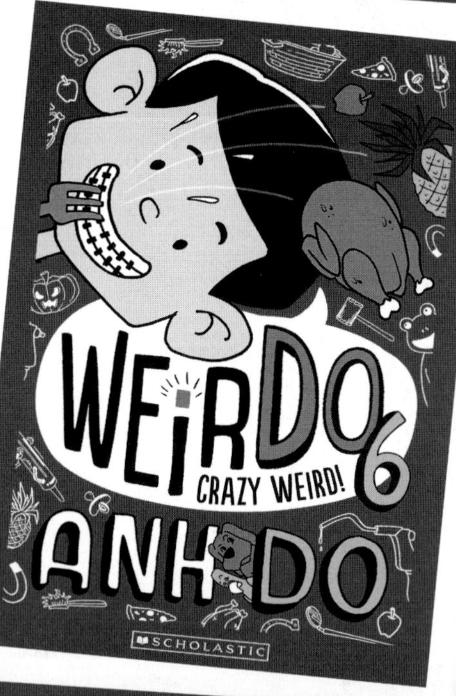

Book 6

GOT IT!

COLLECT THEM ALL!

YOU CAN NEVER HAVE TOO MANY WEIRDOS

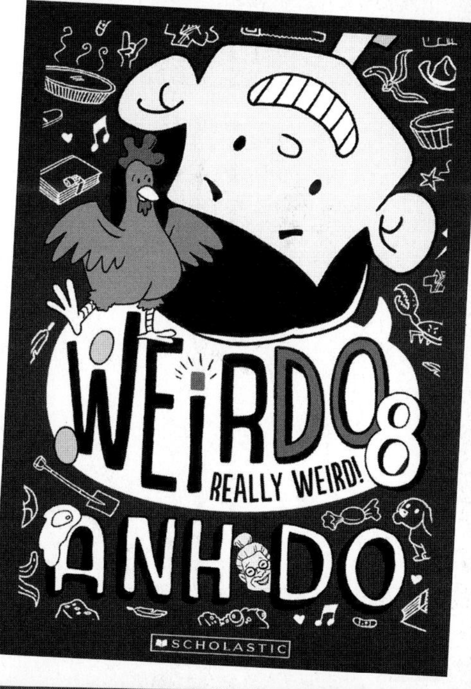

STAY TUNED!